DIGITAL AND INFORMATION LITERACY ™

VIRTUAL REALITY

DON RAUF

rosen publishing's
rosen central®

New York

Published in 2016 by The Rosen Publishing Group, Inc.
29 East 21st Street, New York, NY 10010

Library of Congress Cataloging-in-Publication Data

Rauf, Don, author.
  Virtual reality / Don Rauf. – First edition.
     pages cm. – (Digital and information literacy)
  Audience: Grades 5 to 8.
  ISBN 978-1-4994-3783-6 (library bound) – ISBN 978-1-4994-3781-2 (pbk.)
  – ISBN 978-1-4994-3782-9 (6-pack)
  1. Virtual reality–Juvenile literature. 2. Shared virtual environments–Juvenile literature. 3. Three-dimensional display systems–Juvenile literature. I. Title. II. Series: Digital and information literacy.
  QA76.9.V5R38 2016
  006.8–dc23
                                        2015021638

Manufactured in the United States of America

CONTENTS

INTRODUCTION

"Virtual reality" (VR) is a term used to describe a three-dimensional (3D) computer-generated environment. Virtual realities exist in two different basic formats. Virtual environments can be viewed on a computer screen or with a device that gives complete immersion. The computer user can tour through a 3D landscape using a computer keyboard, mouse, touch screen, joystick, or other type of controller. The Web offers many virtual tours through which visitors can navigate. These can be the interiors of builings, parks, cities, or imaginary worlds. Many games accessed through the Web or computer consoles provide these VR worlds as well. For complete immersion, people can use special goggles or headsets. They can also be in rooms with surround screens. By wearing special goggles, earphones, and possibly special gloves, a person can be totally immersed in a computer-generated world.

Many people are familiar with virtual reality from video games or amusement park attractions. In a virtual environment, a user can experience a universe that resembles the real world we live in or explore an entirely fictional environment—it could be a city far in the future or a landscape all the way back to the time of the dinosaurs. A virtual world may be a different planet, universe, or dimension altogether. No matter what world is created, the user is put in the middle of it all and feels like he or she is actually there.

Virtual reality headsets immerse the wearer in a computer-generated three-dimensional world of images and sounds. Head movements are tracked so a viewer can see a virtual world in every direction.

The uses of virtual reality extend beyond gaming. The military has developed technology to simulate combat conditions and provide training with equipment—such as advanced aircraft and tanks. Scenarios developed for virtual reality can test soldiers' skills and help assure that they are prepared for real battle conditions.

Law enforcement, firefighting, and emergency response professionals may also learn with virtual tech. Educators and scientists have used virtual reality to re-create different worlds—the surfaces of different planets or the inside of a volcano, for example. In medicine, virtual reality can give doctors a 3D view of what it's like inside the heart, lungs, brain, or other parts of the body.

It can provide a look into the body that may help plan a successful surgery and teach surgical techniques as well. In museums and at historical sites, technicians can re-create how a land or village might have looked ages ago. In sports, players can practice and train in a virtual world that presents challenges that will test and further develop their skills.

In construction and architecture, virtual reality enables developers to envision exactly how a facility, office, home, or other structure will look. And in the world of entertainment, there are applications as well, of course, such as interactive cinematic possibilities. Will there be films in the future where you are sitting among the actors or even handing them objects?

This resource gives an understanding of how widespread virtual reality tech is and its diverse uses. You will learn how this technology came to be and how it developed into its current advanced state.

Chapter 1

Welcome to the Virtual World

oogle holds a software developer conference every year called I/O. All attendees receive a gift that is usually something high-tech and high-end, like a laptop, phone, or tablet. Recently, though, Google handed out a piece of cardboard. At first glance, some people thought, how could this possibly be high-tech? Is this a joke? It's just a piece of cardboard. When the piece of cardboard was folded, however, it looked like goggles. The goggles featured lenses and a place to strap in a smartphone. The seemingly simple setup converted a cell phone into a state-of-the-art virtual reality headset.

By looking into this cardboard headset, called Google Cardboard, a user can tour cities in a manner that seems true to life. The wearer can play games or view video content in an immersive way. If the viewer goes to Google Street View, he or she can see the sights of city in three dimensions and look about town with a turn of the head. Google also has a service called Business View, so a person can feel like he or she is visiting a restaurant, office, or department store, for example. With the right app downloaded onto a mobile device, the user can feel like he or she is viewing

Google recently introduced Google Cardboard, a type of low-cost virtual reality goggles that uses smartphones and various apps to enter 3D environments.

a concert in 3D. Volvo created the world's first virtual reality test drive on a smartphone using Google Cardboard. With a turn of the head, the view on the screen changes. A little magnet attachment on the side allows the viewer to click to different screens and websites. Typically, the user will download an app onto his or her smartphone to be able to view different virtual experiences. Users feel like they are looking at an enormous big screen display even though they are using a five-inch device. Another amazing part of this technology: it costs only about $10.

A Window to Different Realities

Google's version of virtual reality has shown the world that the technology does not have to be expensive. Many people are familiar with the technology from an entertaining device created in the twentieth century called the View-Master. The View-Master was first conceived in the 1930s in Portland, Oregon, by William Gruber and Harold Graves. Their viewer had a circular reel that could hold several 3D images. The invention started for educational and military training but quickly became a child's toy, especially when View-Master got the rights to show images of Disney shows. The company produced many Disney-related 3D images, which made the it hugely successful. Disney and View-Master maintain a relationship to the present day.

In a step toward joining the modern world of virtual reality, Mattel (the toy maker that now makes View-Master) has teamed with Google to make a spiffy version of Google's Cardboard goggles. Just like Cardboard, the new View-Master version splits images off of a smartphone to give them a 3D effect. Unlike with the original View-Master, this viewer can spin around and view things in a 360-degree panorama. Users can feel as if they are standing on the Golden Gate Bridge, for example, and look up, down, forward, backward, and side to side—feeling as if they are completely in the world they are viewing. In one display, users can be transported to prehistoric times and feel as if they are among the dinosaurs.

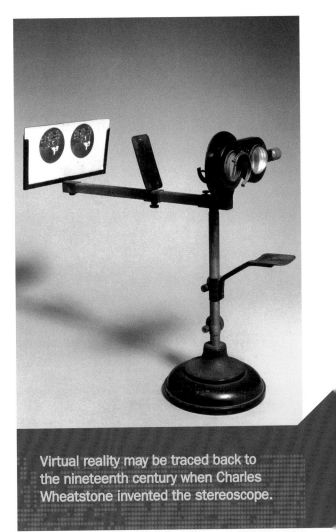

Virtual reality may be traced back to the nineteenth century when Charles Wheatstone invented the stereoscope.

A History of 3D Worlds

The concept of the stereoscope, which is behind the View-Master and Google Cardboard, goes back to 1838. Charles Wheatstone figured out how to use mirrors and angle photos so that two images would come together in a 3D representation. Around the same time, David Brewster created a type of handheld stereoscope viewer that did not depend on mirrors.

In the early 1900s, inventors had figured out different ways to make films with a three-dimensional effect. The world's first 3D feature film was *The Power of Love*, which opened in 1922. More 3D films were made over the decades to come. Many had to be viewed by wearing special red and green cellophane glasses.

The 3D film enjoyed a burst of popularity in the 1950s and early 1960s with movies such as *The House of Wax*, *The Mask*, and even Alfred Hitchcock's *Dial M for Murder*.

Big surround-screen IMAX movies (with surround sound) brought a new level of immersion to 3D films, and viewers could have a more realistic sensation of flying, racing, or other activities through IMAX film. A flurry of renewed interest in 3D came with the release of James Cameron's *Avatar* in 2009, but interest in 3D films has never become as widespread as some have dreamed.

A Step to Full Immersion

As 3D technology was developing, inventors were also thinking of ways to surround people in images and sound so their viewing experiences would be even more realistic. In the 1950s, cinematographer Morton Heilig created a single-viewer console that looked like a type of arcade game. It was called Sensorama. It not only gave a sense of surrounding vision, the machine also had stereo sound and provided other sensations as well. For example, a person in the Sensorama could feel like he or she was riding a motorcycle with a breeze and vibrations from an engine. An odor emitter even gave the user a whiff of different smells while driving through cities or by the ocean.

In the 1980s, scientists created a type of wired glove equipped with sensors that allowed the wearer to more fully interact in a virtual world.

Some have dubbed Heilig the father of virtual reality. Related technology to Sensorama was being used to create simulators to teach how to fly, drive a tank, operate a ship, and drive a car.

File   Edit   View   Favorites   Tools   Help

VIRTUAL REALITY TAKES FLIGHT

Virtual Reality Takes Flight

One of the practical uses of virtual reality has been flight simulation to train pilots. The idea goes back to the early days of flight. Even in World War I, engineers were putting together contraptions to train pilots how to fly, attempting to re-create the flying experience with an earthbound machine.

In the 1920s and 1930s, Edwin Link of Binghamton, New York, refined the flight simulator and built a thriving business selling simulators to the military. The simulators could re-create motions and have the appropriate panels, gauges, and controls. But at the time, they lacked the screens or visual feedback to make it seem like a pilot in training was actually in the air.

In the 1950s and 1960s, inventors incorporated films shot from real airplanes. This was a step toward virtual reality, but the options presented to a training pilot were limited.

By the 1970s, the technology advanced with computer-generated images (CGI). In 1971, the McDonnell-Douglas Electronics Corporation introduced a system called Vital II (Virtual Image Takeoff and Landing). This gave a very realistic representation of runways at night. The machine displayed directional lights, flashing lights or beacons, and runway lights.

The Federal Aviation Administration approved the technology, and pilots received early training on how to take off and land with the Vital II. Over the next three decades, the virtual reality of flying became more and more sophisticated and realistic.

In 1961, engineers at Philco Corporation came up with the first head-mounted display (HMD). People wearing the device would change the view of what they were seeing simply by shifting their heads. The HMD was originally linked to closed-circuit cameras that would allow the wearer to view a real location remotely. In 1965, Ivan Sutherland, a computer scientist, was dreaming up 3D virtual worlds and figured out how to use the HMD to view such environments. The early VR headgear, however, was huge and heavy. His virtual headset had to be supported by a mechanical arm or it would crush the wearer. NASA, however, was very interested in this technology and funded its development. NASA first applied the technology to more realistic flight simulation.

Bringing VR into the Home

In the mid-1980s, scientists were figuring out ways to combine virtual reality technology with home computers. Innovators were also perfecting the wired glove, sometimes called the data glove. The glove was built with sensors that could send information to a computer. Gestures and hand motions could be read by the computer. Eventually, this type of tech could be incorporated into other VR technologies to make even more realistic experiences. A person viewing a virtual world now had the ability to "pick up" or "move" items in that fictional place. The virtual revolution had begun.

13

Chapter 2

Game On! Being Part of the Action

As computer graphics became better and better from the 1970s onward, a natural place to use them was in the world of computer gaming. In the 1980s, Sega (originally short for Service Games) introduced a type of headset that allowed players to have a 3D effect in games such as *Space Harrier* and *Maze Hunter*. Other 3D games came along, but it was the creation of vast virtual worlds that were revolutionary.

Computer game designers created entire new worlds that people could explore, usually by using an avatar. An avatar is a character that represents the user on the screen. A player directs the avatar to walk, run, look around, or even fly. Through the Internet, people have had a chance to enter virtual worlds and interact with other people (or avatars).

LucasFilm Games may be the first company to introduce a virtual world online with its creation called *Habitat*. It was developed for the Commodore 64 computer in 1987. Many players could access the *Habitat* universe through their home computers. When many different

Habitat, a game developed by LucasFilm, was one of the first multiparticipant online environments. Users interacted in this virtual world through avatars, or representations of themselves.

players can access a Web-based world and interact, it is called a massive multiplayer universe (MMU).

Living in Cyberspace

Virtual worlds have evolved. One of the most popular virtual worlds today is *Second Life*, which was introduced in 2003 by Linden Labs in San Francisco. *Second Life* is not a game. People explore this world, acting as if they are in a real world. They communicate with other avatars who are there. The avatars play games, go to clubs, and just hang out. They buy land and build homes. People can work in this world and earn Linden dollars to buy art, clothes, and other items. This money system has connected to the real world—Linden dollars can actually be exchanged for real dollars. On the other hand, a person can use a credit card or real money to buy more Linden dollars.

Real companies such as Sony, Nike, and Toyota advertise or have stores in *Second Life*. Businesses even hold meetings there. Real-life employees send their avatars and gather in a virtual conference room. It's like a conference call but in the virtual world of *Second Life*. There is even a *Second Life* Shakespeare Company that performs works of Shakespeare in this virtual realm.

Some online virtual worlds allow viewers to interact with other users through their computers. In *Second Life*, users socialize, play, build houses, work jobs, and more.

Kaneva and *IMVU* are other online services like *Second Life*. They also offer 3D environments to meet new people and interact. *The Sims* is related to these other virtual worlds in that it simulates real life. In *Sims*, the user directs characters to interact. The player moves characters around and has them do simple things like wash, dress, and eat. The characters can buy things such as furniture and decorations.

Minecraft has been another popular 3D world, especially among younger people. Here players can build homes with blocks, electrify them, and battle monsters. Multiple players can join forces through the Internet and work together.

Massively Multiplayer Action

More and more virtual worlds are being born through games. *World of Warcraft*, created by Blizzard Entertainment, is hugely popular, with more than ten million players. It has also been one of the biggest moneymakers, bringing in billions of dollars. Players use avatars to interact with other players, fight monsters, and go on quests.

Another smash-hit game, *Halo*, takes players to a virtual universe five hundred years in the future where they fight alien invaders, among other things.

Other top games that feature virtual worlds include *Assassin's Creed, Call of Duty, Fallout, Grand Theft Auto,* and *Prince of Persia*. Although they are not always multiplayer, games that simulate real sports have their own virtual worlds, and they cover pretty much all the major sports, including football, basketball, soccer, and golf.

Capturing Body Motions

Technology that translates a body's motion to actions on a screen can make these virtual worlds seem even more real. Nintendo Wii (pronounced "wee") may be one of the best-known examples of this type of motion-capture. The Wii uses wireless motion-sensor technology. The Wii user holds a device in

17

Motion sensors have made it easier to "move" in virtual worlds. Nintendo Wii's game console translates physical motion to motion on screen. Here a player tries a "virtual" golf swing.

hand called the Wii remote that allow a player to have his or her physical motions translated into onscreen actions.

In a Wii virtual tennis game, a player swings his arm as if hitting a tennis ball and the image on screen replicates that motion. If a Wii player moves her arm as if throwing a bowling ball down the alley, the ball on screen moves to correspond with the player's motion.

Wii also introduced a balance board that plugs into the system so users can simulate skiing, snowboarding, skateboarding, or surfing. Wii realized that there are a number of physical activities that can be translated in fitness using its technology and offers many workouts under the title of Wii Fit—including more unusual activities such as super hula hoop and tightrope walking.

The Gloves Are On

The wired glove, or "data glove," is another motion-capture technology that was designed to make the virtual world more real. By wearing the glove, the user would become more a part of the action on the screen. The idea was that a person's hand in the real world would become a hand in the cyber world.

While not enabling the user to feel things, it could touch and move things on screen. One of the earliest versions, the Nintendo Power Glove appeared in the late 1980s for home use. One of the original games made for the glove involved grabbing a cyber ball and throwing it at colorful bricks. The technology at first was awkward. The ball, for instance, was hard to direct. It didn't always go where the thrower wanted.

Today, wired gloves and motion/gesture-capture systems are much more sensitive. For example, the IGS glove from Synertia/Animazoo claims to capture motion within a tenth of a degree. The new breed of data gloves are designed to provide total intuitive interaction with 3D games and virtual environments. Motion sensor technology is receiving a lot of praise because it's getting video game players to do something they might not ordinarily do: move their bodies and get a little exercise.

We've Got You Surrounded

With 3D worlds and motion capture being perfected, gaming engineers also wanted people to feel more immersed in the games with total surrounding vision. In the mid-1990s, Nintendo introduced a type of headset for 3D gaming called Virtual Boy, but the technology was still primitive. Users

19

Virtual reality technology has made computer game play more realistic. Wearing headsets and using game controllers, players can run, jump, shoot, and compete against other players in a virtual environment.

complained that it made them feel queasy, and the company stopped selling the product.

Some arcade games in the 1990s were also attempting to build artificial worlds. Players could step into oversized pods, put on virtual goggles (or often an oversized helmet), and feel immersed in the games. With a plastic gun or phaser, a player could shoot into a virtual world.

Virtual reality rides have been perfected. For example, Universal Studios in Los Angeles has a *Simpsons* ride that features a runaway roller coaster. Fun seekers enter this pod and strap in. The pod swerves and jerks

File   Edit   View   Favorites   Tools   Help

THE YOUNG WHIZ BEHIND A VIRTUAL REVOLUTION

The Young Whiz Behind a Virtual Revolution

Palmer Luckey was born in 1992 in Long Beach, California. He loved to tinker with things. From ages eleven to sixteen, he devoted much of his time to building his own personal computer. He collected virtual reality headsets and became obsessed with building his own VR goggles.

In 2012, at age twenty, he dropped out of college and formed OculusVR to build his virtual reality glasses. He started it as a crowd-funded project through the website Kickstarter. At first, he saw his VR glasses as a passion project, and he didn't expect to make much money. He wrote that he hoped to have $10 profit left over when it was all completed so he could buy a celebratory pizza. But some tech giants took notice, and they began chipping in. The world took notice. He quickly raised $2.5 million.

His headsets cost about $350. They were far from perfect but better than anything that had come before. It took him just a year to come up with a new and improved version of the headsets he called Oculus Rift. A frenzy has built around his new technology with investors, computer engineers, and game developers all clamoring to be part of the action.

Then in 2014, Facebook came knocking. It bought Luckey's new company for $2 billion. Mark Zuckerberg, the creator of Facebook, has envisioned a future Facebook as a cyber universe where avatars do their social networking while walking down virtual streets rather than texting.

about on hydraulics as riders view fast-paced 3D images that make it feel as though they are racing through a crazy carnival. Many other amusement park rides operate on that virtual technology—although like some real-life rides, these can cause people to feel sick to their stomachs.

After decades, the idea of practical and satisfying virtual reality headsets had seemed to fizzle out. But in 2012, a new VR headset came along that reignited an interest in virtual reality. The new technology, called Oculus Rift, was far superior to anything that had come before. "It is one of those rare products where describing it in mere words doesn't come anywhere near to realistically depicting how incredible the experience of wearing one is," wrote Jim Edwards in *Business Insider*. "It's disconcertingly good—the internal 3D world moves as convincingly as the real one."

Oculus Rift is one of the most advanced virtual reality headsets to date. Palmer Luckey invented the virtual goggles, and Facebook bought his company for $2 billion when he was just twenty-one years old.

One of Oculus Rift's biggest selling points: it's not nauseating. The new Oculus technology has been opening up new worlds of realistic gaming and entertainments, ranging from harrowing virtual roller coaster rides to space exploration. One tech reviewer has raved about a seemingly simple game called *Euro Truck Simulator 2*. The headset provides such realistic visuals that he tried to hang his arm outside of an imaginary driver's window as he motored along. When the game is modified with a force feedback steering wheel, the player can feel the rumble of the highway.

Technologies such as Oculus Rift are examples of how virtual worlds are getting closer and closer to simulating the real thing.

MYTHS & FACTS

MYTH Virtual reality equipment is expensive.

FACT Not always. The technology for virtual reality continues to improve and prices continue to drop. Look at Google Cardboard's VR goggles. They cost just about $10.

MYTH Virtual reality is a passing fad.

FACT VR does seem to go through bursts of interest and then fade away. There is renewed interest in the technology today. The fact is, interest may sometimes disappear, but people eventually return to the concept and it continues to develop.

MYTH Virtual reality will replace real life.

FACT While more time might be spent in virtual worlds, a person cannot eat a virtual hamburger or breathe virtual air. We still need to live in the real world.

Chapter 3

Solving Real-World Problems

hile the gaming world is huge when it comes to virtual reality, the technology is being applied for many real-world practical purposes. VR has been used for training purposes and, in particular, teaching people how to pilot different vehicles.

Building Military Might

The military has long been interested in VR to train soldiers on various vehicles and equipment. Some of these are very expensive, so the military wants soldiers to be able to operate them properly and maintain them. In some ways, the idea of VR military training for aircraft today is similar to the early Link trainers. The idea is to get accustomed to the feel of the plane and all the instruments aboard and how they operate. With today's technology, the pilot can move his or her head and see just about anywhere outside the plane. Soldiers can also virtually learn how to launch torpedoes and operate heavy artillery.

The military also uses VR to simulate battle situations. In recent years, the army has been testing the Dismounted Soldier Training System. With

Today, soldiers can train and test their skills in simulated battle conditions. Wearing head-mounted displays with microphones, soldiers can interact and communicate with other members of their squad.

this state-of-the-art VR gear, soldiers are put in a room with computer backpacks and multiple sensors to track their movements. They hold replica weapons that are wired into the system. They view different combat scenarios through their headsets. A commander can arrange different battle elements in the virtual worlds, including weather, number of combatants, and time of day. The scenes are designed to help soldiers refine their shooting, moving, decision making, and communication. In some military testing, soldiers may encounter hidden explosives, dust storms, smoke, sand, a loss of communication, and other obstacles.

Virtual training also extends into more subtle areas. The military has been developing simulated scenarios to help soldiers interact better with people from different cultures. Basically, a soldier can role-play with a virtual villager and learn customs to improve interactions. How much eye contact is appropriate? How close do you stand near someone? What do a person's verbal and nonverbal actions mean?

The military has also created VR games designed to help recruit new soldiers. For example, the army produced *America's Army,* which is a shooter game with a number of 3D battle scenarios. Apparently, the game has been hugely successful at attracting new recruits.

A Helping Hand for Health Care

VR is a common tool for training medical professionals. It has proven to be effective in honing the skills of surgeons. With a computer-generated display of the human body and organs, a surgeon in training can master methods without doing any harm to a patient. Some of the VR surgery programs measure tissue damage, and students can get an idea of how well they are performing based on this. Doctors can practice feeding small tubes up virtual blood vessels to get a better handle on performing surgery. They can remove computer-generated tumors. Dentists can practice filling cavities in 3D cyber mouths. Using avatars, health professionals can practice interacting with others on a health care team. In fact, some nurses have gone through simulated professional interactions using *Second Life*. Paramedics can also run through potential scenarios of accidents and learn how to react in such high-pressure situations.

Technology is being used to develop immersive situations that can help patients with physical rehabilitation. Those with injured or weakened limbs, for example, may use exercises and games involving gesture-control technology, similar to the Wii.

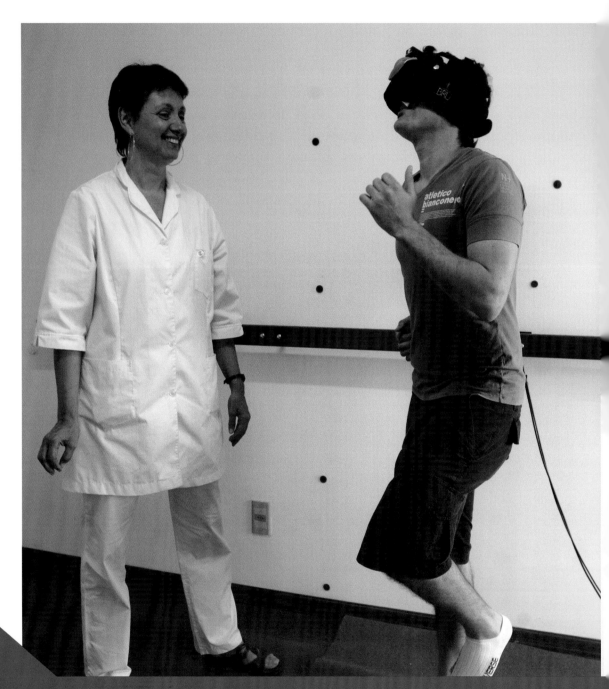

The health care industry has put virtual reality technology to practical use. Patients can perform physical rehabilitation by completing virtual exercises and games.

Scientists have found that virtual worlds may also help with pain management. A project from the University of Washington called SnowWorld showed computer-generated snowy and cold scenes to patients who had third-degree burns. Wearing headsets, the patients were floating through landscapes filled with snow, snowmen, icebergs, penguins, and igloos. Researchers have found that these patients reduced their pain by 50 to 90 percent—they, in effect, traveled away from their pain in their minds.

VR is proving to be a practical way to treat phobias, including fear of flying (aerophobia), fear of spiders (arachnophobia), and fear of closed spaces (claustrophobia). The technology can provide safe environments to challenge patients' thoughts and behaviors and help them overcome the obstacles. The technology has been used to treat autism as well. In one cyber exercise, an autistic child puts on a headset and enters a computer-generated classroom with avatar teachers and students. Autistic patients may have trouble paying attention. The avatars give presentations but they start to fade away if the viewer's attention drifts.

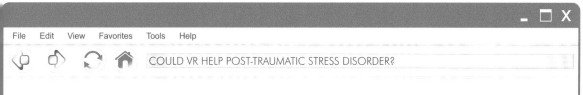

File　Edit　View　Favorites　Tools　Help

COULD VR HELP POST-TRAUMATIC STRESS DISORDER?

Could VR Help Post-Traumatic Stress Disorder?

Post-traumatic stress disorder (PTSD) happens to some soldiers who have been through life-threatening combat situations. It is a trauma that patients carry with them. They may experience nightmares, flashbacks, sleep difficulties, anxieties, and stress. Recent studies have shown that virtual reality exercises that allow soldiers or veterans with PTSD to relive the traumatic experiences may help relieve the condition. One soldier said that by reliving his traumatic events in a virtual environment, he didn't have to think about them when he was at home with his family.

A Way to Engage and Educate

VR has been able to engage students in a dramatic way. Lessons about the universe can be much more compelling if people can travel through solar systems, past stars and planets. Learning about dinosaurs may certainly be more interesting if a person can walk among them. Students now have the potential to feel as if they are underwater to learn about oceanography or even inside volcanoes or the center of the earth.

Students can also walk among ancient lands and civilizations. These are experiences that many museums and galleries may also want to offer their visitors through advances in virtual technology. Using special laser scanning techniques, the Science Museum of London was able to preserve a 3D version of its popular shipping gallery exhibit. The exhibit no longer physically exists but visitors can still see a 3D representation of the entire gallery.

Many, Many Applications

For athletes, virtual technology has brought a new way to train, again using motion sensors similar to the Wii. One interesting application in this area is for cyclists. With the right setup, cyclists can connect stationary bikes to sensors that feed into a computer and then connect to a massively multiplayer online game where they can race on various terrains against any number of different cyclists.

In the world of fashion, some envision a world where designs can be displayed on avatar models who walk down virtual runways. Topshop, the London fashion retailer, gave customers a chance to put on headsets and transport themselves to a live-streamed London Fashion Week catwalk. These customers had 360-degree vision of the event so they could choose what they were viewing.

For business applications, companies have held meetings in *Second Life* and even advertised in these computer-generated worlds. In some businesses, being able to "walk through" a computer model can be helpful. Architects, construction workers, and engineers can use the technology to thoroughly review the plans they have for homes, bridges, office buildings, and other

Virtual reality technology can provide a safe, efficient, and cost-effective way to train people for risky activities. Parachute simulators let jumpers practice without taking to the air.

structures. Ford, the auto manufacturer, has its Ford Virtual Reality Center. Building virtual models can be much cheaper than building physical models. Computer engineers can create virtual cars and easily adjust height, width, length, color, and all other elements that go into a car's design to see what works best and makes it most appealing.

VR has possibilities in almost every industry. As the technology improves and the prices for VR drop, people are envisioning more applications for this technology.

TEN GREAT QUESTIONS

TO ASK A VIRTUAL REALITY DESIGNER OR ENGINEE

1   How did you get interested in the field?

2   What courses should I study in high school that can help me find a job?

3   What was your first experience with virtual reality?

4   What do you find rewarding about working in virtual reality?

5 What do you dislike about virtual reality?

6   What are a couple of ways I might experience virtual reality?

7   What are the biggest challenges in your job?

8   What current virtual reality applications do you especially like?

9   What would be a good way to explore careers in virtual reality?

10   What are some ways virtual reality might be used in the future?

Chapter 4

Stepping into the Future

Microsoft recently joined in on the excitement that has been growing around new virtual reality technology. It introduced the HoloLens, a device that seemed to be pulled directly from science fiction. In the movie *Minority Report*, Tom Cruise's character interacts with screens and information that seem to appear in midair (without wearing a headset). He can simply use his hands to move these screens around in his field of vision or quickly sweep them away with a brush of the hand.

That idea is very similar to the HoloLens. When wearers put on this headset, they can see various screens, icons, and virtual objects floating before them while still viewing the real world as well. The objects are superimposed over their field of vision. So these items seem to appear in the real-life setting, wherever the user happens to be. The headset operates with motion control. The viewer can, for example, click on the Internet with a midair flick of the hand. Scientists have dubbed this technology "augmented reality."

Maybe the wearer wants to fix a clogged sink. The HoloLens would let this person access an online pipe repair video that appears to float in the

Microsoft's HoloLens melds the virtual with the real. Here, a plumber instructs how to fix a pipe with video and other computer elements that appear before the HoloLens wearer.

air. The wearer can still see the real-world pipe that needs to be fixed. So in this type of virtual reality, the user isn't transported to another world, but computer elements are brought into the real world.

The wearer can video chat with someone face-to-face while walking around the house. The person talking could circle something he asks about in the house, and the HoloLens wearer will see that real object circled.

Microsoft now owns *Minecraft*, the super popular virtual-world-building game. The headset lets you build with *Minecraft* blocks wherever you are. For example, you can start building a structure on your coffee table or it can seem as if you're breaking through a Minecraft wall in your home hallway. As of this writing, the HoloLens is not available for purchase by the general public, yet Microsoft anticipates that it will be ready for purchase within a couple years.

In some ways, another new product that has also been in the demonstration stage is similar. It is called Magic Leap. This new headset also promises the viewer access to website and desktop apps via airborne icons. Magic Leap is funded by Google. Experts believe there will be a competition going between the two products when they become available to the public. In either case, both headsets show how ideas that were once considered far off in the future may soon be a reality.

Where Is Virtual Reality Heading?

Some envision a world where virtual reality is so real that we will not have to commute to the office to have an office work experience. People can sit at home as their avatars check into work. In the world of entertainment, people may be able to buy tickets to concerts or sporting events that basically transport them to the event without them ever leaving home.

Feature films may be created in which viewers feel like they are walking among the characters and sitting in the rooms where they are performing. A traveler may simply be able to put on a headset and take off on a restful holiday rather than spend time and money on getting to a destination.

In the movie *Transcendence*, Johnny Depp downloads his mind into a computer. Some believe that goal may one day be achievable and conscious beings could live practically forever in a virtual world.

Learning to How to Create Future Worlds

The Electronic Visualization Lab at the University of Illinois, Chicago, is one of the best-known virtual reality institutes in the world. And the technology coming out of that facility is pushing virtual reality into the future. In the 2000s, the group perfected the CAVE Automatic Virtual Environment with

A cave automatic virtual environment (CAVE) is a room full of rear-projection screens. Viewers with special glasses can walk around and study 3D images from different angles in a CAVE.

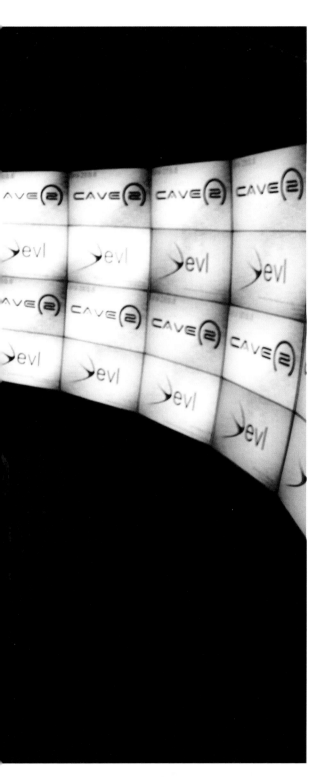

the highest resolution display wall on the planet. In effect, it's a room that puts a person in a virtual world. The Electronic Visualization Lab works with people in many different disciplines—art, earth sciences, learning sciences, medical research, and communications, to name a few. It is working on Project Lifelike to create realistic virtual humans (avatars). It is trying to create avatars that look, sound, and react like real people.

Students who train and take classes at the Electronic Visualization Lab have access to innovative technology that will one day be commonplace. This learning environment encourages the students to play with and experiment with the technology to explore its possibilities to solve real-world problems.

Other colleges in addition to the University of Illinois are offering courses that help train students in the skills needed to develop virtual reality technology. The University of Idaho offers a bachelor's degree in Virtual Technology and Design.

VIRTUAL REALITY ON THE BIG SCREEN

Virtual Reality on the Big Screen

As a teenager, Palmer Luckey, who invented the Oculus Rift VR headset, was inspired by the movies *The Matrix* and *The Lawnmower Man*, which envisioned what virtual reality might do. Facebook, which bought Oculus Rift, is developing movies specifically to be viewed in this VR environment, and other companies are following this path as well. Here are a few Hollywood productions that have imagined the potential of VR.

Ender's Game (2013). Ender Wiggin, a twelve-year-old, and other young cadets play advanced virtual war games to prepare for battle with alien space fleets.

Source Code (2011). Jake Gyllenhaal portrays an army pilot who finds himself resurrected in a type of virtual reality to stop a would-be bomber.

Life 2.0 (2011). A documentary about those who use avatars and create cyber lives for themselves in the online world of *Second Life*.

Inception (2010). Leonardo DiCaprio projects himself into a virtual environment made up of the dreams of other people.

Courses may include digital modeling, computer-aided design, computer animation, three-dimensional design, multimedia, computer programming, software development, human-computer interaction, virtual environments, and virtual reality design.

In high school and middle school, students interested in this field can benefit by taking classes in math, science, computer science, physics, and art. Virtual reality technology requires serious knowledge of computers but it also requires imagination, so courses that promote creativity are important.

In an article in the *Pacific Standard*, architect Mark Foster Gage pointed out the great potential virtual reality has to open new worlds: "There are colors we haven't yet discovered, forms we've never imagined, and sounds nobody has ever heard. All suddenly possible to truly experience through virtual reality."

GLOSSARY

augmented reality Technology that superimposes computer-generated images over the viewer's field of vision.

avatar An icon or figure that represents a real person in a computer game or computer environment.

cyber Relating to computers, information technology, or virtual reality.

data glove A device that looks like a glove and is intended to ease interaction in a virtual world by letting simple hand motions control actions in a computer-generated environment.

digital modeling Constructing virtual 3D objects with computer software.

gesture-control technology Computer systems that can interpret human body movement.

IMAX From Image Maximum, IMAX is a widescreen cinema technique.

massively multiplayer online game Internet game that allows large numbers of players to join in and interact.

panorama A wide view, often 360 degrees.

smartphone A cellular phone that offers many functions of a computer, camera, and other devices.

social networking Websites and applications dedicated to connecting people for professional or personal reasons.

stereoscope A device that brings together two images of the same thing taken at slightly different angles to create one image that appears to have three dimensions or depth.

FOR MORE INFORMATION

Canadian Advanced Technology Alliance (CATA)
207 Bank Street, Suite 416
Ottawa, ON K2P 2N2
Canada
(613) 236-6550
Website: http://www.cata.ca
The largest high-tech association in Canada, CATA is a comprehensive
    resource for the latest high-tech news in Canada.

Canadian Association for Computer Science
5090 Explorer Drive, Suite 801
Mississauga, ON L4W 4T9
Canada
(905) 602-1370
Website: http://www.cips.ca
Information is provided here for those pursuing or advancing a career in
    computer science or software engineering.

Information Technology Association of Canada
220 Laurier Avenue West, Suite 1120
Ottawa, ON K1P 5Z9
Canada
(613) 238-4822
Website: http://itac.ca
This organization focuses on business issues related to information technol-
    ogy in Canada. The site features news for professionals about
    computer software and electronic services.

Institute of Electrical and Electronics Engineers/Computer Society
2001 L Street NW, Suite 700
Washington, DC 20036-4928
(202) 371-0101
Website: http://www.computer.org
The world's leading membership organization dedicated to computer science and technology offers information, networking, and career-development resources.

International Virtual Reality Photography Association
Website: http://ivrpa.org
This is an international association of professionals who create and produce 360-degree interactive, immersive images, also called 360-degree panoramas. Members include professional photographers, programmers, web developers, designers, and software developers who produce and use 360-degree imaging techniques.

Websites
Because of the changing nature of Internet links, Rosen Publishing has developed an online list of websites related to the subject of this book. This site is update regularly. Please use this link to access the list.

http://www.rosenlinks.com/DIL/Virt

FOR FURTHER READING

Blascovich, Jim, and Jeremy Bailenson. *Infinite Reality: Avatars, Eternal Life, New Worlds, and the Dawn of the Virtual Revolution*. New York, NY: HarperCollins, 2011.

Buckley, Patrick. *Virtual Reality Beginner's Guide + Google Cardboard Inspired VR Viewer*. New York, NY: Regan Arts, 2014.

Cline, Ernest. *Ready Player One: A Novel*. New York, NY: Broadway Books, 2012.

Cudworth, Ann Latham. *Virtual World Design*. Natick, MA: A K Peters/CRC Press, 2014.

Dashner, James. *The Eye of Minds*. New York, NY: Ember/Random House, 2014.

Davis, Bradley Austin, Karen Bryla, and Phillips Alexander Benton. *Oculus Rift in Action*. Greenwich, CT: Manning Publications, 2014.

Haller, Mark. *Emerging Technologies of Augmented Reality: Interfaces and Design*. Hershey, PA: Igi Publishing, 2011.

Kipper, Gregg. *Augmented Reality: An Emerging Technologies Guide to AR*. Rockland, MA: Syngress Media, 2013.

Nite, Sky. *Virtual Reality Insider: Guidebook for the VR Industry*. Swansea, UK: New Dimension Entertainment, 2014.

Parisi, Tony. *Learning Virtual Reality: Developing Immersive Experiences and Applications for Desktop, Web, and Mobile*. Sebastapol, CA: O'Reilly Media, 2015.

Robbins, Sarah, and Mark Bell. *Second Life for Dummies*. Hoboken, NJ: For Dummies/Wiley, 2008.

Schroeder, Ralph. *Being There Together: Social Interaction in Shared Virtual Environments*. New York, NY: Human Technology Interaction, 2010.

BIBLIOGRAPHY

Blascovich, Jim, and Jeremy Bailenson. *Infinite Reality: Avatars, Eternal Life, New Worlds, and the Dawn of the Virtual Revolution*. New York City: HarperCollins, 2011.

Chayka, Kyle. "What Will We Do with Virtual Reality?" *Pacific Standard*, March 27, 2015. Retrieved April 30, 2015 (http://www.psmag.com/nature-and-technology/what-will-we-do-with-virtual-reality).

Edwards, Jim. "Mere Words Can't Do Justice to How Awesome It Is Inside the Oculus Rift Gaming Headset Facebook Just Bought." *Business Insider*, March 25, 2014. Retrieved April 30, 2015 (http://www.businessinsider.com/what-its-like-using-oculus-rift-2014-3).

Finley, Klint. "Could Immersive Virtual Reality Tech Solve World Problems?" *Slate*, March 5, 2015. Retrieved April 30, 2015 (http://www.slate.com/blogs/future_tense/2015/03/05/virtual_reality_technology_could_address_anxiety_ptsd_and_phobias_will_we.html).

Heffernen, Virginia. "Virtual Reality Fails Its Way to Success." *New York Times*, November 14, 2014. Retrieved April 30, 2015 (http://www.nytimes.com/2014/11/16/magazine/virtual-reality-fails-its-way-to-success.html?_r=1).

Levy, Karyn. "Second Life Has Devolved into a Post-Apocalyptic Virtual World, and the Weirdest Thing Is How Many People Still Use It." *Business Insider*, August 1, 2014. Retrieved April 30, 2015 (http://www.businessinsider.com/second-life-today-2014-7).

Murdock, Josh. "Virtual Reality Made Simple with Google Cardboard." ProfessorJosh.com, April 4, 2015. Retrieved April 30, 2015 (http://professorjosh.com/2015/04/04/virtual-reality-made-simple-with-google-cardboard).

Parkin, Simon. "The Best Virtual-Reality Experience so Far." *MIT Technology Review*, March 17, 2015. Retrieved April 30, 2015 (http://www.

technologyreview.com/view/535941/
the-best-virtual-reality-experience-so-far).

Statt, Nick. "Microsoft's HoloLens Explained: How It Works and Why It's Different." C|Net, January 24, 2015. Retrieved April 30, 2015 (http://www.cnet.com/news/microsoft-hololens-explained-how-it-works-and-why-its-different).

Statt, Nick. "Virtual Reality Is Taking over the Video Game Industry." C|Net, February 28, 2015. Retrieved April 30, 2015 (http://www.cnet.com/news/virtual-reality-is-taking-over-the-video-game-industry).

Strangman, Nicole, and Tracey Hall. *Virtual Reality/Simulations*. Wakefield, MA: National Center on Accessible Instructional Materials, 2013.

Virtual Reality Society. "Virtual Reality." Retrieved April 30, 2015 (http://www.vrs.org.uk).

INDEX

About the Author

Don Rauf is the author of several technology books for young adults including *Kickstarter, Killer Lipstick and Other Spy Gadgets, Getting the Most Out of Makerspaces to Explore Arduino and Electronics, Getting the Most Out of Makerspaces to Build Unmanned Aerial Vehicles,* and *Powering Up a Career in Internet Security.*

Photo Credits

Cover, p. 1 (inset, left to right) Alexandru Nika/Shutterstock.com, Mike Kiev/iStock/Thinkstock, grafvision/Shutterstock.com, Rommel Canlas/Shutterstock.com; pp. 5, 8 Bloomberg/Getty Images; p. 9 Science & Society Picture Library/Getty Images; p. 11 James King-Holmes/W Industries/Science Source; p. 15 Sascha Steinbach/Getty Images; p. 16 Stephane De Sakutin/AFP/Getty Images; pp. 18, 36-37 © AP Images; p. 20 Marty Katz/The LIFE Image Collection/Getty Images; p. 22 Stefano Tinti/Shutterstock.com; p. 26 U.S. Army photo by VIS Markus Rauchenberger; p. 28 Miguel Rojo/AFP/Getty Images; p. 31 Press Association/AP Images; p. 34 Rex Features/AP Images; cover and interior pages (pixels) © iStockphoto.com/suprun

Designer: Nicole Russo; Editor: Nicholas Croce;
Photo Researcher: Karen Huang